Rembrandt

The Christmas Story

REMBRANDT

THE CHRISTMAS STORY

THOMAS NELSON PUBLISHERS

Nashville

Published in Nashville, Tennessee, by Thomas Nelson, Inc.

The Bible version used in this publication is THE NEW KING JAMES VERSION. Copyright © 1979, 1980, 1982, Thomas Nelson, Inc., Publishers.

Library of Congress Cataloging-in-Publication Data

Rembrandt Harmenszoon van Rijn, 1606–1669.
    Rembrandt : the Christmas story.
       p.   cm.
    Works by Rembrandt accompanied by selections from the New King James Version of the Gospels.
    ISBN 0-7852-7464-2 (hc)
    1. Rembrandt Harmenszoon van Rijn, 1606–1669 — Themes, motives. 2. Jesus Christ — Nativity — Art. I. Bible, N.T. Gospels. English. New King James. Selections. 1998. II. Title.
ND653.R4R36 1998
759.9492–dc21   97-53274
                                                     CIP

Printed in Singapore.

CONTENTS

INTRODUCTION

This little book contains the story of the birth of Jesus, the Savior of the world. It is the greatest story ever told. The events in this story, which affects all mankind, actually took place in Roman-occupied Palestine some two thousand years ago.

We celebrate this story every Christmas as we remember those events of long ago, so beautifully depicted in the Gospels, particularly the Gospel of Luke. Since those events were first recorded many years ago, there have been many translations of the Gospels. We have chosen the New King James Version for its literary beauty and its contemporary appeal.

These classic texts have inspired countless millions throughout the ages. They have also appealed to — and inspired — many artists, possibly none as much as Rembrandt. Over half of his life's work was devoted to painting images directly inspired by the pages of the Bible he clearly loved and knew so well. Rembrandt's father was a staunch Calvinist, and his son's education was strict yet thorough. However, Rembrandt left school at a young age to start what was to become a great career.

This book focuses on some thirty-four images centered around the birth of Jesus, from the Annunciation to Simeon's prophecy. Some events, such as the adoration of the shepherds and the wise men, are well known; others much less so. All, as will be seen, are interpreted with love, adoration, and awe at the greatest mystery and gift of all: God's gift of His Son to an unsuspecting world.

The rest of the Introduction is devoted to some background information on some of the pictures that are executed in different styles, from large oil paintings to more intimate pen and ink sketches and some black-and-white prints, originally destined for commercial reproduction. This is followed by the simple juxtaposition of Rembrandt's images and the Gospel text that moved and inspired him.

MARY VISITS ELIZABETH

In this beautiful scene Rembrandt uses imagination and sets the encounter outside the rather palatial front door of the house of Zacharias the priest. The focus of the painting—and indeed the light—falls upon a beautifully young and serene Mary being greeted by her elderly cousin Elizabeth as dusk falls. A servant removes Mary's coat while another servant leads away the donkey on which she made the journey. Old Zacharias is also keen to welcome Mary: he appears, however, to have some difficulty in walking and needs to lean on the shoulder of a young boy in order to get down his front steps.

THE BIRTH OF JESUS

The beautiful and sensitive pen and ink wash chosen to illustrate the birth is devoid of outside detail. It simply shows Mary holding her newborn baby against her shoulder in an attitude of great tenderness and love.

Rembrandt cannot have drawn this scene from his imagination. Perhaps he used his wife, Saskia, with one of their children as a model. Based upon the date of the drawing this would have been their first child, a son named Rumbartus who was baptized on December 16, 1635. Sadly the little boy lived for only two months.

Their next two children would also die very young, and only Titus, their fourth child, born in September 1641, was to survive. Rembrandt clearly knew the pain and the joy of childbirth, and the fact that most of his paintings of the holy family date from this period says something about his inspiration and identification with the theme of the supreme gift of new life.

The Shepherds Worship the Child

There are two large canvases on this theme, both painted in the same year and both featured in this book. Both are lit by a single invisible light that seems to come from the baby Jesus Himself. He is clearly the center of attention and the most miraculous baby ever. Both feature the simple surroundings of a stable such as Rembrandt would have been familiar with in his native Holland.

Both paintings are remarkable, not by the detail of the surroundings but by the sense of awe and worship evident in the faces and body language of the simple shepherds, here to worship their Savior.

The Flight into Egypt

Rembrandt made a lot of the dramatic nature of the flight into Egypt. The angel speaking to Joseph in a dream, the hurried departure, the stealthy flight by night to escape any prying eyes, the tiring nature of the journey of more than one hundred miles, the need to rest and find sustenance, the campfire at night . . .

It was a theme he was to return to often. Rembrandt was particularly captivated by the play of light and shadow—and the nighttime journey provided the opportunity for many trials using different techniques. One of his most successful was this delightful oil, where Joseph and Mary are seen on the shore of a pool in which they are reflected while a third person, possibly a shepherd, tends a fire, the warm glow of which illuminates the landscape.

In this majestic painting, one of Rembrandt's earliest masterpieces, the scene is set in the great temple at Jerusalem at the foot of a broad flight of stairs, presumably leading to the high priest to whom the child would be presented.

Rembrandt chose to depict a moment before the presentation. The light streaming into the cavernous building is focused on the white-haired Simeon with Jesus in his arms. Mary looks on in surprise while Joseph, also kneeling, holds the two doves for the sacrifice, as prescribed by the Law. We only have a back view of the most prominent figure, whose arms are raised. We can only presume she is Anna, the prophetess, who has also just recognized the child as the long-promised Messiah.

The second oil depicting Simeon dates from the last year of Rembrandt's life and demonstrates his continuing fascination with the nature of worship. This unfinished painting focuses on the depth of emotion of the gray-haired old man, tenderly holding the child in his stiff arms in an attitude of great reverence. The painting is Rembrandt's last known work, a fitting testament executed by an old man who had always been captivated by the baby from Bethlehem, whom he was soon going to meet.

The subject of Jesus' early years, about which the Gospels are silent, captivated Rembrandt. The intimacy of a loving family carefully caring for a much-loved only son was dear to his heart—for deeply personal reasons.

Many illustrations of peaceful domestic scenes exist: the baby fast asleep in his wickerwork cradle; Mary breast-feeding the infant; Joseph at work in the carpenter's shop; and quiet evening scenes with Mary and Joseph and sometimes other people.

This particular scene shows Mary reading to her aunt Elizabeth, who appears to have fallen asleep. Her hands, however, are still holding the cord with which she rocked the baby to sleep. The light, from a hidden source, draws the eye to Mary, sharply outlining her profile, and casting a large shadow of Elizabeth on the wall. This seems to repeat Mary's silhouette on a larger scale, so that the figures of the two women appear to flow together in one large shadow that rises above the child as if to protect Him.

David Wavre

The Annunciation of the Angel Gabriel to Mary

Pen and ink drawing; 14.4 x 12.4 cm; 1635.
Besançon, Musée des Beaux-Arts.

THE ANNUNCIATION

Now in the sixth month the angel Gabriel was sent by God to a city of Galilee named Nazareth, to a virgin betrothed to a man whose name was Joseph, of the house of David. The virgin's name was Mary. And having come in, the angel said to her, "Rejoice, highly favored one, the Lord is with you; blessed are you among women!"

But when she saw him, she was troubled at his saying, and considered what manner of greeting this was. Then the angel said to her, "Do not be afraid, Mary, for you have found favor with God. And behold, you will conceive in your womb and bring forth a Son, and shall call His name JESUS. He will be great, and will be called the Son of the Highest; and the Lord God will give Him the throne of His father David. And He will reign over the house of Jacob forever, and of His kingdom there will be no end."

Then Mary said to the angel, "How can this be, since I do not know a man?"

And the angel answered and said to her, "The Holy Spirit will come upon you, and the power of the Highest will overshadow you; therefore, also, that Holy One who is to be born will be called the Son of God. Now indeed, Elizabeth your relative has also conceived a son in her old age; and this is now the sixth month for her who was called barren. For with God nothing will be impossible."

Then Mary said, "Behold the maidservant of the Lord! Let it be to me according to your word." And the angel departed from her.

Luke 1:26–38

MARY VISITS ELIZABETH

Now Mary arose in those days and went into the hill country with haste, to a city of Judah, and entered the house of Zacharias and greeted Elizabeth. And it happened, when Elizabeth heard the greeting of Mary, that the babe leaped in her womb; and Elizabeth was filled with the Holy Spirit. Then she spoke out with a loud voice and said, "Blessed are you among women, and blessed is the fruit of your womb! But why is this granted to me, that the mother of my Lord should come to me? For indeed, as soon as the voice of your greeting sounded in my ears, the babe leaped in my womb for joy. Blessed is she who believed, for there will be a fulfillment of those things which were told her from the Lord."

And Mary said:

> "My soul magnifies the Lord,
> And my spirit has rejoiced in God my Savior.
> For He has regarded the lowly state of His
>   maidservant;
> For behold, henceforth all generations will call me
>   blessed.
> For He who is mighty has done great things for me,
> And holy is His name.

Mary's visit to Elizabeth

Oil on panel rounded at top; 57 x 48 cm; 1640.
Detroit, The Detroit Institute of Art.

20

And His mercy is on those who fear Him
From generation to generation.
He has shown strength with His arm;
He has scattered the proud in the imagination of
   their hearts.
He has put down the mighty from their thrones,
And exalted the lowly.
He has filled the hungry with good things,
And the rich He has sent away empty.
He has helped His servant Israel,
In remembrance of His mercy,
As He spoke to our fathers,
To Abraham and to his seed forever."

And Mary remained with her about three months, and returned to her house.

Luke 1:39–56

Mary's visit to Elizabeth (detail)

JOHN THE BAPTIST IS BORN

Now Elizabeth's full time came for her to be delivered, and she brought forth a son. When her neighbors and relatives heard how the Lord had shown great mercy to her, they rejoiced with her.

So it was, on the eighth day, that they came to circumcise the child; and they would have called him by the name of his father, Zacharias. His mother answered and said, "No; he shall be called John."

But they said to her, "There is no one among your relatives who is called by this name."

So they made signs to his father—what he would have him called. And he asked for a writing tablet, and wrote, saying, "His name is John." So they all marveled. Immediately his mouth was opened and his tongue loosed, and he spoke, praising God. Then fear came on all who dwelt around them; and all these sayings were discussed throughout all the hill country of Judea. And all those who heard them kept them in their hearts, saying, "What kind of child will this be?" And the hand of the Lord was with him.

Now his father Zacharias was filled with the Holy spirit, and prophesied, saying:

"Blessed is the Lord God of Israel,
For He has visited and redeemed His people,
And has raised up a horn of salvation for us
In the house of His servant David,
As He spoke by the mouth of His holy prophets,
Who have been since the world began,
That we should be saved from our enemies

And from the hand of all who hate us,
To perform the mercy promised to our fathers
And to remember His holy covenant,
The oath which He swore to our father Abraham:
To grant us that we,
Being delivered from the hand of our enemies,
Might serve Him without fear,
In holiness and righteousness before Him all the
    days of our life.

"And you, child, will be called the prophet of the
    Highest;
For you will go before the face of the Lord to
    prepare His ways,
To give knowledge of salvation to His people
By the remission of their sins,
Through the tender mercy of our God,
With which the Dayspring from on high has
    visited us;
To give light to those who sit in darkness and the
    shadow of death,
To guide our feet into the way of peace."

So the child grew and became strong in spirit, and was
in the deserts till the day of his manifestation to Israel.

Luke 1:57–80

The naming of St. John the Baptist

Pen and brush drawing; 19.9 x 31.4 cm; 1644.
Paris, The Louvre.

THE BIRTH OF JESUS

And it came to pass in those days that a decree went out from Caesar Augustus that all the world should be registered. This census first took place while Quirinius was governing Syria. So all went to be registered, everyone to his own city.

Joseph also went up from Galilee, out of the city of Nazareth, into Judea, to the city of David, which is called Bethlehem, because he was of the house and lineage of David, to be registered with Mary, his betrothed wife, who was with child. So it was, that while they were there, the days were completed for her to be delivered. And she brought forth her firstborn Son, and wrapped Him in swaddling cloths, and laid Him in a manger, because there was no room for them in the inn.

Luke 2:1–7

Mary with the child by a window

Pen and brush drawing; 15.5 x 13.7 cm; ca. 1635. London, British Museum.

The Angel Appears to the Shepherds

Now there were in the same country shepherds living out in the fields, keeping watch over their flock by night. And behold, an angel of the Lord stood before them, and the glory of the Lord shone around them, and they were greatly afraid. Then the angel said to them, "Do not be afraid, for behold, I bring you good tidings of great joy which will be to all people. For there is born to you this day in the city of David a Savior, who is Christ the Lord. And this will be the sign to you: You will find a Babe wrapped in swaddling cloths, lying in a manger."

And suddenly there was with the angel a multitude of the heavenly host praising God and saying:

> "Glory to God in the highest,
> And on earth peace, goodwill toward men!"
>
> Luke 2:8–14

The angel appears to the shepherds

Etching; 26.2 x 21.8 cm; 1634.
Amsterdam, Rijksprentenkabinet.

30

The angel appears to the shepherds (opposite)

Pen and brush drawing; 17.6 x 20 cm; ca. 1640– 42.
Hamburg, Kunsthalle.

The angel appears to the shepherds (below)

Pen and brush drawing; 18.8 x 28 cm; ca. 1655.
Amsterdam, Rijksprentenkabinet.

THE SHEPHERDS WORSHIP THE CHILD

So it was, when the angels had gone away from them into heaven, that the shepherds said to one another, "Let us now go to Bethlehem and see this thing that has come to pass, which the Lord has made known to us."

And they came with haste and found Mary and Joseph, and the Babe lying in a manger. Now when they had seen Him, they made widely known the saying which was told them concerning this Child. And all those who heard it marveled at those things which were told them by the shepherds. But Mary kept all these things and pondered them in her heart. Then the shepherds returned, glorifying and praising God for all the things that they had heard and seen, as it was told them.

Luke 2:15–20

The shepherds worship the child

Oil on canvas; 65.5 x 55 cm; 1646.
London, National Gallery.

34

The shepherds worship the child (opposite)

Oil on canvas; 97 x 71.5 cm; 1646.
Munich, Alte Pinakothek.

The shepherds worship the child (below)

Etching; 10.5 x 12.9 cm; 1654.
Amsterdam, Rijksprentenkabinet.

The shepherds worship the child (above)

Etching; 14.8 x 19.8 cm; ca. 1652.
Amsterdam, Rijksprentenkabinet.

The shepherds worship the child (detail)

Oil on canvas; 65.5 x 55 cm; 1646.
London, National Gallery.

THE CIRCUMCISION

A nd when eight days were completed for the circumcision of the Child, His name was called JESUS, the name given by the angel before He was conceived in the womb.

Luke 2:21

The circumcision (opposite)
Oil on canvas; 56.6 x 75 cm; 1661.
Washington, National Gallery of Art, Widener Collection.

The circumcision
Etching; 8.4 x 6.4 cm; ca. 1630.
London, British Museum.

40

THE ADORATION OF THE WISE MEN

Now after Jesus was born in Bethlehem of Judea in the days of Herod the king, behold, wise men from the East came to Jerusalem, saying, "Where is He who has been born King of the Jews? For we have seen His star in the East and have come to worship Him."

When Herod the king heard this, he was troubled, and all Jerusalem with him. And when he had gathered all the chief priests and scribes of the people together, he inquired of them where the Christ was to be born.

The adoration of the wise men

Oil on paper on canvas; 45 x 39 cm; 1632.
St. Petersburg, The Hermitage.

So they said to him, "In Bethlehem of Judea, for thus it is written by the prophet:

> 'But you, Bethlehem, in the land of Judah,
> Are not the least among the rulers of Judah;
> For out of you shall come a Ruler
> Who will shepherd My people Israel.' "

Then Herod, when he had secretly called the wise men, determined from them what time the star appeared. And he sent them to Bethlehem and said, "Go and search carefully for the young Child, and when you have found Him, bring back word to me, that I may come and worship Him also."

Matthew 2:1– 8

The adoration of the wise men (detail)

Oil on paper on canvas; 45 x 39 cm; 1632.
St. Petersburg, The Hermitage.

43

W hen they heard the king, they departed; and behold, the star which they had seen in the East went before them, till it came and stood over where the young Child was. When they saw the star, they rejoiced with exceedingly great joy. And when they had come into the house, they saw the young Child with Mary His mother, and fell down and worshiped Him. And when they had opened their treasures, they presented gifts to Him: gold, frankincense, and myrrh. Then, being divinely warned in a dream that they should not return to Herod, they departed for their own country another way.

Matthew 2:9–12

The adoration of the Magi

Pen and ink drawing; 17.4 x 22.8 cm; ca. 1638. Berlin, Kupferstichkabinett der Staatlichen Museen.

45

THE ANGEL APPEARS TO JOSEPH

Now when they had departed, behold, an angel of the Lord appeared to Joseph in a dream, saying, "Arise, take the young Child and His mother, flee to Egypt, and stay there until I bring you word; for Herod will seek the young Child to destroy Him."

Matthew 2:13

The angel appears to Joseph in a dream

Oil on panel; 20 x 27 cm; 1645.
Berlin, Gemaldegalerie der Staatlichen Museen.

The angel appears to Joseph in a dream

Pen and brush drawing; 17.9 x 18.1 cm; ca. 1652.
Amsterdam, Rijksprentenkabinet.

The angel appears to Joseph in a dream

Pen and brush drawing; 14.5 x 18.7 cm; ca. 1650.
Berlin, Kupferstichkabinett der Staatlichen Museen.

THE FLIGHT INTO EGYPT

When he [Joseph] arose, he took the young Child and His mother by night and departed for Egypt, and was there until the death of Herod, that it might be fulfilled which was spoken by the Lord through the prophet, saying, "Out of Egypt I called My Son."

Matthew 2:14–15

The flight into Egypt

Oil on panel; 26.5 x 24 cm; 1627.
Tours, Musée des Beaux-Arts.

The flight into Egypt

Etching; 21.2 x 28.4 cm; ca. 1653.
Amsterdam, Rijksprentenkabinet.

The flight into Egypt

Etching; 8.9 x 6.2 cm; 1633.
Amsterdam, Rijksprentenkabinet.

The flight into Egypt

Etching; 12.8 x 11 cm; 1651.
London, British Museum.

The rest on the flight into Egypt

Oil on panel; 34 x 47 cm; 1647.
Dublin, National Gallery of Ireland.

55

The rest on the flight into Egypt

Etching; 9.2 x 5.9 cm; 1644.
Amsterdam, Rijksprentenkabinet.

Resuming the journey after the rest on the flight into Egypt

Pen and brush drawing; 19.3 x 24.1 cm; ca. 1652.
Berlin, Kupferstichkabinett der Staatlichen Museen.

THE SONG OF SIMEON

Now when the days of her [Mary's] purification according to the law of Moses were completed, they brought Him to Jerusalem to present Him to the Lord (as it is written in the law of the Lord, "Every male who opens the womb shall be called holy to the LORD"), and to offer a sacrifice according to what is said in the law of the Lord, "A pair of turtledoves or two young pigeons."

And behold, there was a man in Jerusalem whose name was Simeon, and this man was just and devout, waiting for the Consolation of Israel, and the Holy Spirit was upon him. And it had been revealed to him by the Holy Spirit that he would not see death before he had seen the Lord's Christ.

The song of Simeon

Oil on canvas; 99 x 78.5 cm; 1669.
Stockholm, Nationalmuseum.

So he came by the Spirit into the temple. And when the parents brought in the Child Jesus, to do for Him according to the custom of the law, he took Him up in his arms and blessed God and said:

"Lord, now You are letting Your servant depart
   in peace,
According to Your word;
For my eyes have seen Your salvation
Which You have prepared before the face of all
   peoples,
A light to bring revelation to the Gentiles,
And the glory of Your people Israel."

Luke 2:22–32

The song of Simeon

Oil on panel; 61 x 48 cm; 1631.
The Hague, Mauritshuis.

SIMEON'S PROPHECY

And Joseph and His mother marveled at those things which were spoken of Him. Then Simeon blessed them, and said to Mary His mother, "Behold, this Child is destined for the fall and rising of many in Israel, and for a sign which will be spoken against (yes, a sword will pierce through your own soul also), that the thoughts of many hearts may be revealed."

Luke 2:33–35

Simeon's prophecy to Mary (detail)

Oil on panel; 55.5 x 44 cm; 1628.
Hamburg, Kunsthalle.

The song of Simeon

Pen and ink drawing; 18 x 19 cm; ca. 1640.
Amsterdam, Amsterdams Historisch Museum.

The song of Simeon

Pen and brush drawing; 12 x 8.9 cm; 1661.
The Hague, Koninklijke Bibliotheek.

65

THE PROPHETESS ANNA

Now there was one, Anna, a prophetess, the daughter of Phanuel, of the tribe of Asher. She was of a great age, and had lived with a husband seven years from her virginity; and this woman was a widow of about eighty-four years, who did not depart from the temple, but served God with fastings and prayers night and day. And coming in that instant she gave thanks to the Lord, and spoke of Him to all those who looked for redemption in Jerusalem.

Luke 2:36–38

Simeon's prophecy to Mary (opposite)

Oil on panel; 55.5 x 44 cm; 1628.
Hamburg, Kunsthalle.

Simeon's prophecy to Mary

Etching; 10.3 x 7.8 cm; 1630.
Amsterdam, Rijksprentenkabinet.

THE CHILD GREW IN WISDOM

So when they had performed all things according to the law of the Lord, they returned to Galilee, to their own city, Nazareth.

And the Child grew and became strong in spirit, filled with wisdom; and the grace of God was upon Him.

Luke 2:39–40

The holy family

Oil on panel; 45 x 47 cm; 1646.
Kassel, Gemaldegallerie.

The holy family in the evening

Oil on panel; 66.5 x 78 cm;
ca. 1644.
Amsterdam, Rijksmuseum.

The Infant in a crib

Oil on canvas; 117 x 91 cm; 1645.
St. Petersburg, The Hermitage.